WALLOON WRITERS REVIEW

FIFTH EDITION

Founded from a deep passion for Northern Michigan and the Upper Peninsula, *Walloon Writers Review* was created to offer a place where Michigan writers and photographers could share their Up North stories, poetry, photography and reflections upon one of the most inspiring places in the world. So many are touched by this region, from summer cottages, family vacations, residents, seasonal residents, students, those who make annual treks up here for their favorite season. *Walloon Writers Review* welcomes those creative writers and photographers, whether published several times over or just starting out and regardless of current location. The feeling and memories of Northern Michigan and the UP never leave you.

We are honored to have **Glen Young** as our Associate Editor for our Fifth Anniversary Edition.

Glen Young is a teacher, writer, kayak guide, and house painter. His poetry has appeared in *Walloon Writers Review*, as well as the anthologies *Beneath the Lilac Canopy* and *Thoreau at Mackinac*. He is a founding member of the Foundation for Teaching and Learning, as well as the Little Traverse Literary Guild. He serves on the board of the Harbor Springs Festival of the Book and the Mackinac Arts Council. He divides his time between Petoskey and Mackinac Island in northern Michigan.

Keep up with us at www.walloonwritersreview.com and on social media!

WALLOON WRITERS REVIEW
P.O. Box 2460
Petoskey, MI 49770
editor@walloonwriters.com

Editor: Jennifer Huder
Associate Editor: Glen Young
Cover Photography: Sunrise - Higgins Lake ©Melissa Seitz
Produced by MissionPointPress.com

Walloon Writers Review (ISSN 2572-9683)

ISBN: 978-1-950659-31-9
Library of Congress Control Number: 2019917194

CONTENTS

THE BIRTH OF AGATES ... Raymond Luczak ... 6

SUPERIOR NIGHT ... David Anthony Sam ... 7

TWO-HEARTED ... David Anthony Sam ... 8

DAWN BESIDE BLACK LAKE ... David Anthony Sam ... 9

SHIFTING SANDS ... Helen Raica-Klotz ... 10

Sunrise Whitefish Point ... Melissa Seitz ... 12

DRAGONFLIES ... Raymond Luczak ... 14

PAINT RIVER ... Edd Tury ... 15

LAKE MICHIGAN MORNING ... Edd Tury ... 15

Impressionism ... Charles Rammelkamp ... 16

COLD & FREE ... Steve Hooper ... 17

MICHIGAN AMBITION ... Joyce Brinkman ... 18

THE PROPERTY AT LEVERING ... Deda Kavanagh ... 19

The Approach ... Grace Giroux ... 20

EVER A FIREFLY ... Robert Vivian ... 22

Torch Lake Fox ... Steven W. Huder ... 23

NORTHERN TIME ... Steve Ullom ... 24

DO YOU REMEMBER? ... Steve Ullom ... 25

THE SMELL OF HEX ... Tim Chilcote ... 26

Sweet Northern Friend ... Kelly Tingle Kazmierski ... 29

THE MAN BY THE RIVER ... Rick Fowler ... 30

TOGETHER (Lake Michigan dune, 2019) ... Jan Shoemaker ... 33

JULY 4 ... Phillip Sterling ... 34

JULY IS TO RELATIVE AS SAILOR IS TO FAMILY ...
Phillip Sterling ... 35

OCTOBER SPEAKS OF DIGNITY ... Phillip Sterling ... 36

A RELIGIOUS EXPERIENCE ... John Lennon ... 37

ELK RAPIDS SUNSET ... Shelley Smithson ... 38

DIVIDEND ENOUGH ... Glen Young ... 39

PORCH POEM ... Taylor Tucker ... 40

89 STEPS ... Rick Fowler ... 41

***Flag Poin*t** ... Taylor Tucker ... 44

Wings of Wonder ... Kelly Tingle Kazmierski ... 46

REVISION ... DeDa Kavanagh ... 48

STAG ... Ellen Lord ... 49

A HAIKU TRILOGY FOR A MICHIGAN SUMMER ...
Ellen Lord ... 50

Northern Lights ... Kelly Tingle Kazmierski ... 52

THE GIFT OF THE TIN BOX ... Nancy Renko ... 54

Sunrise Brockway Mountain ... Melissa Seitz ... 58

RELIQUARY ... Greg Rappleye ... 60

**IN A DREAM, MY FATHER
DECIDES TO GO ICE FISHING** ... Greg Rappye ... 61

SEARCHING FOR SUNLIGHT ... John Lennon ... 62

GRAND TRAVERSE IN WHITE ... Edd Tury ... 63

ROCKER ... Skip Renker ... 64

Treasure Island ... Taylor Tucker ... 65

I MIGHT RIDE OFF ... Skip Renker ... 66

DECEMBER 23, NORTHERN MICHIGAN ... CJ Giroux ... 67

MUD SEASON ... Edy Stoughton ... 68

EXPOSURE ... Melissa Seitz ... 70

GUARDIANS OF THE NORTHERN LAKES ... Amy Zaranek ... 72

17th Annual Crooked Tree Arts Center Juried Young Writers Exposition
First Place Winners of Poetry and Prose from Elementary, Middle & High School ... 83

CONTRIBUTORS ... 97

WALLOON WRITERS REVIEW

FIFTH EDITION

THE BIRTH OF AGATES

RAYMOND LUCZAK

Ghosts dress in only gray and white.
This is how they camouflage their volcanic selves.
Lake Superior is bottled with them.
You can't see them but they move like fish.
They streak lightnings of iced lava.
Their whispers startle walleye and lake sturgeon.
They lurk in the shadow of fishing boats.
Their folds flit around the swaying bait.
They dream of toying with the line.
Laughter from above ripples like thunder.
Their eyes turn dull as yellow perch.
They shed tears of crimson rainbows.
It hurts to wipe away these unfulfilled dreams.
The shores of Lake Superior bloom in agate.

SUPERIOR NIGHT

DAVID ANTHONY SAM

Silence threads the rivermouth,
blackening with night,
as sparks fly from the fire
at my blistered, bleeding feet.

Seeking solace in the woods
near the shore of Superior,
I think of betrayals
and dream of resolutions.

Pine needles pillow the hard
ground. My body seeks
a comfortable place in the silence
that frosts a glaze of moonlight.

My dreams still walk the backtrails
and the lakeshore sands.
Quiet enters me,
murmuring like black waves.

TWO-HEARTED

DAVID ANTHONY SAM

Superior wind blew landward
across the sand and round-rocked beach,
up the thirty feet of bank,
dragging smoke from the low fire
back into the quiet trees.

They sat as invaders beside their fire,
eyes burning from the acrid smoke,
studying the dark center of flames,
minds on the morning and the long
trail through the woods–

The trail cut by the Coast Guard
through the trees planted by the CCC
because all Michigan had been scalped
clean by the lumberers–that was the path
that waited in darkness tonight.

Two miles to Two Heart.
The wind spoke to them.
The flames answered.
They knew it.
They listened.

DAWN BESIDE BLACK LAKE

DAVID ANTHONY SAM

The cold lake exhales mist into warm air.
The cry of the loon laughs at dawn.

A whirring in the brush as birds take flight.
The cry of the loon laughs at dawn.

I wake from sleep, damp with dew.
The cry of the loon laughs at dawn.

Mist rises, drawn by the sun into oblivion
and the blue sky called heaven.

The cry of the loon laughs at dawn.

SHIFTING SANDS

HELEN RAICA-KLOTZ

"You can always go home again, but you can't go back all the way."
-Bob Dylan, "Mississippi"

I don't know what Torch Lake looked like before the mines dumped the residue from the copper on its shores, creating miles of black gritty sand that stung my eyes and burned my nose every time the wind blew hard. And the wind would blow through our small town in Michigan's Upper Peninsula, the sand coating our house a quarter mile away from the lake. A fine grey paste would cover the window panes that my mother would attack every spring and fall with Windex and her Finnish work ethic. "I scrub and scrub, but I can never keep this place clean," she'd complain. The rags she used would take two washings, with bleach, to come clean.

As a child, I didn't know any of this. The black sands were not pollution and waste, not an environmental hazard. To me, the sands were just there, had always been there, like our Zenith television and our Ford Pinto and my dad's limp when it rained.

I would walk Gypsy, our mixed breed dog, over the railroad tracks and down the hill to the sands almost every summer day. We would wander aimlessly, meandering our way along the shifting surface. The sands were like crystallized coal, shattered and scattered in a million pieces that covered the shoreline and surrounding landscape. In the summer, the sands were hot, unbelievably so, pure black drenched in sunlight with no shade anywhere. The local university tried to grow grasses and trees here without much success. Whether it was lack of knowledge about the sands' topography or lack of any real funding, after a few years, the project stopped. Occasionally, I would run into a dead tree on my walks, brown and bowed over by the stiff winds, roots still clinging to the barren landscape.

My dog and I would walk down to the lake, where fish with tumors the size of my fist would swim. At least, that's what my grizzled old neighbor Kurt Haukula told me, between drags on his Camel cigarette. "All that sand gave those fish cancer. Can't eat a damn one." I never saw any fish. I only saw the black water. It was different than the sands: it moved, ebbing up to the shore in small ripples, ever shifting and glinting in the light. It wasn't really black either, not thick and viscous, not dirty. It was clear and clean, stretched across the surface like saran wrap, through which you could see down below to the black sand underneath. What was further out, where the bottom disappeared into darkness? I don't know. There were sudden drop-offs, dangerous currents in the lake, and I was made to promise never, ever to swim out there. Of course, some kids did – older, daring boys. Me, I was content to walk with my dog around its edges, staring at its vastness. The lake stretched for miles, emptying past a scrubby tree line into the Houghton Canal. A huge distance to a ten-year old, without a boat or any swimming ability to speak of. It whispered of possibilities to me, of things just beyond the surface of my life in this small Upper Peninsula town.

Of course, all this was a long time ago. My dog died, hit by a pick-up one snowy January, and I hit adolescence. I discovered boys, far more interesting than the curve of black and water that stretched along the horizon. The sands moved to the periphery of my vision, glimpsed as I sped by in a car, on to other, more exciting places.

I went back to visit my father ten years ago. I wanted to take my son to the sands, the place where I spent so much of my time when I was his age. We walked across the road, over the tracks. My son grumbled: "How much further?" And then we were there. A ten-foot fence surrounded the sands, stretching out in either direction. Signs were posted every hundred feet that read, "PRIVATE PROPERTY, KEEP OUT." I stared. My son was nonplussed. "Can we go home and play on the computer now?" At dinner, I ask my father about this new development. "Some rich guy downstate bought it all. Gonna sell it as waterfront property." I smile, waiting for the punch line. After a long pause, he continues. "Sold three lots already."

Later that night, I returned alone. I walked the periphery of the fence, running my fingers against the metal grids. It was getting dark and harder to see. As I squinted my eyes and looked into the distance, I couldn't tell where the sands ended and the water began.

Sunrise Whitefish Point ©Melissa Seitz

DRAGONFLIES

RAYMOND LUCZAK

Spin us another thread in the air
where dead mosquitoes knot,
stitching up our nightly quilts,
squared of hunger and hunt,
swinging from the clotheslines
between dawn and dusk.

We nymph from egg to adulthood,
blessed with the innate gift to sew.
Four months are all what we've got.
We bustle about, buzzing gossip and tips
as we weave through the cattails.
Life is a constant state fair.

Come September we will die.
It'll be too cold for mosquitoes to flit
like the lazy beer drinkers that they are.
We soon starve our energy to browse.
Fireflies punctuate our funerals.
The swamp is an empty fairground.

Flaps of our wings disintegrate,
ripped pieces of fabric floating
past mallards judging one more time
before that tarp of snow and ice
submerges our prize-winning handiwork.
Spring thaw is our favorite needle.

PAINT RIVER

EDD TURY

A gunshot echoes
from a distant ridge.
November's last leaf separates,
hesitates,
tumbles to earth.
A black wolf turns its head to watch.
Gray clouds skitter
on the northwest wind.

LAKE MICHIGAN MORNING

EDD TURY

The lake appears viscous
            like clear blue honey
its rocky bottom seems
            close enough to touch

We slide into the mist
            smooth surface yielding
            our paddles dipping, dripping

Beyond the fog a freighter's engine
            thumps its low song

Quiet solitude
            cathedral of sky and water

Every breath
            a prayer

Impressionism ©Charles Rammelkamp

COLD & FREE

STEVE HOOPER

From *If You Seek a Pleasant Peninsula by Under This Cold Sky.*

There's a light on the water
The sky is an author
A ghost writer of our stories and times
Though we call this place home
It's never our own
Our livelihood, logging and mines

But is her land expendable,
Her yields dependable?
A profit that soon will run dry
For all the waters deep inland;
Superior, Huron, and Michigan
Give life to the land and the sky

Cold and free
Is the North wind over fresh water seas
Tranquil and low
December fields of lake effect snow
Calm and still
Nightfall and the July whippoorwill
So won't you tell me - Do you want to see this land remain pristine?
Our lakes and our rivers run clean?
Do you want to see this land remain pristine?

This place is not replaceable
Nor history untraceable
Do we care what we leave when we're gone?
But for now all I offer
Despite the world and its bothers
Someday will be a song

MICHIGAN AMBITION

JOYCE BRINKMAN

When I grow up, I want to be
the librarian on Mackinac Island.
Frigid winter days, I'll want to feed
the fire with chunks of wood to keep
the reading patrons warm.

Then staring out one, tall, glass pane
besides the teal-tiled fireplace, I'll see
through drifting snow the icy lake,
and tame my tongue's dry run
of devouring walnut fudge.

THE PROPERTY AT LEVERING

DEDA KAVANAGH

Dad finagled the land up north
from Mom's inheritance.

Then he sculpted it in a wild way.
The Macintosh orchard suns itself on a little hill.
The dappled, weed-whacked path
leads you to the pond with water skaters,
called Jesus bugs.
He claimed the boys "borrowed" a beaver
to get it started.
The swamp where women didn't go,
is left intact, is witness,
still hosts brothers with rifles and orange jackets.
There's a building site near the fishing hole.
He drilled, found water,
and that would fit the bill.

The house never went up.
Seems the ground he fostered
was the home he built.

The Approach ©Grace Giroux

EVER A FIREFLY

ROBERT VIVIAN

Ever a firefly circa the later summer evening, bright now then fading away, ever Tina's sandals that cradle her little feet, ever a firefly one then another then another then all gone suddenly nowhere to be seen but felt in keen flaring of felt aftermath and the shooting of stars in our blood, Michigan fireflies and waves of Lake Michigan, all the rivers I have ever waded who somehow wade in me, ever a rising fish and ever the uptick in rapt wonder this causes every time, every boil, ever the cast you or I make in brief looping parabola of glory given by the moon, by the laws of physics, by the soul's deep laughter and sobs of weeping, oh, all the world is a loving roundness, a perfect sphere, bodies of so much water they flow into and out of each other always, weathered docks and peeling paint, the slap of a wave against the boards or the hull of a boat, the dragon flies and the strident song of the cicadas crying out that all of this is passing, all of this is precious and beautiful—ever a firefly, ever a heartbeat, ever a desire to write a poem and breathe a poem with one's whole being, ever the need to say I love you, ever to touch and hold a stranger's hand, ever to seal an envelope with a sloppy kiss and thereby send a kiss airborne into the ether out into the world, oh, what precious summer we are, what fleeting shadows of desire, the sun going down on all of us as the fires bank down into embers as we wonder and we pray what austerity or gentleness is waiting for us where we listen and we die and we listen again, hoping to see a firefly glow because it can, because it must.

Torch Lake Fox ©Steven W. Huder

NORTHERN TIME

STEVE ULLOM

passing like a steady clock
measured in the sound of
pushed wave hitting waiting shore
followed by
pushed wave hitting waiting shore.
The muscles of the lake
stretching and contracting,
spraying stray moisture in the air
landing in jagged rock fissures
slowly spreading open to a cold yellow sun
exposing roots extending new green shoots,
desperate footholds
not to be taken for granted.

High above
dark feathers bristle on stretching wing
sharp beak and eye slipping through the wind
scanning fissures and small spaces
under the emerald trees
counting out the time remaining
for something only it will know
in its own good time
above pushed wave
hitting waiting shore.

DO YOU REMEMBER?

STEVE ULLOM

We walked the North beach together
so many years ago,
sand-smitten wind blowing our hair
to match the day's rebellions,
our feet hopping from boulder,
placed by giants in a drunken prank,
to another, placed by contractors
in drunken greed,
all gray granite and smoky quartz.
In retrospect,
it seemed the most solid footing
we ever had.
Off the boulders, if we looked back
we'd see our footsteps and the shore itself
leaking back to the superior water.

Rock, beach, our lives -
shaped by time and tides.
Larger waves occasionally splashed up,
gossipy white frothing
around the scuffed thick rubber
of canvass tennis shoes
(hiking shoes, for us, were unknown then).
A cold slap always made us laugh,
sharp barks of courage
by those able to dream forward.

Do we each have something of our dreams now,
whether day-dreamed or night-whispered?
It doesn't matter, I guess.
I just wondered if you knew
the lake was still there,
dreaming eternity.

THE SMELL OF HEX

TIM CHILCOTE

The ad man would pitch it like this:
[in your throatiest whisper]
HEX: *Pulsating with electric potential*

Apply fragrance liberally to neck, face—
And a spritz for the waders

Parfum de hexagenia limbata
Earthy accord of jurassic mayflies
Dark top notes of silted river bottom
Cut by sand-filtered spring water
And humid cedar-swamp base

Options for magazine spreads:

> Wide-angle shot of solitary angler
> Trout rises clean from the water
> Pounds a deadeye dead drift
> *You'll be hooked*
>
> Kype-jawed fisherman
> Fly-rod as conquering damascus blade
> Fawning damsel in state of undress
> *She'll be hooked*
>
> No more fisherman
> Close-up of trophy brown poised to feed
> In the fish's eye
> Faint reflection of semi-clothed damsel
> *The bite is on*

Pitch for thirty-second television spot:

> Three nights of beard stubble and barbed hooks
> Stench of stogies, sweat and *Deep Woods*
> *Off!* Nothing a double-shot of HEX can't fix
> The bedside clock reads 4:00 a.m.
> The nymph—or [ahem] damsel—asks
> *Catch anything... yet?*

Integrated social media promotion:

> Insta-pic of bearded hero
> Vintage pickup backed to river's edge
> Brand-y-est seven-weight rod-reel combo
> Well-weathered retriever atop rotomolded cooler
> [set up casting call for geriatric dogs]
> *'Like' all four items for the chance to be entered to win*
> *the fishing trip of a lifetime*

Client isn't having any of this shit

Scrap everything

Send creative on a full product immersion

Headspace technology to
Capture and analyze the molecules

Hear the humming veined wings
Point your headlamp skyward
Screech at mass of mayflies
Attacking lumens and eclipsing the moon
Alight on vest, waders, glasses, your teeth

Eau de end of days
Forget aroma and mesmerizing aldehydes

Gasp and heave your line
Factory of floating fishflies
Browns slurping, mouths agape
Rising, flopping, wallowing in the scent

Hook a speckled 25-incher
To hell with the photo
Brain the fish and slit the belly—
Engorged stomach shameless with insects
Pitch innards in river—
Seed the beaver's castoreum glands

Return to creative review
Distill the extract to the core

The rebrand goes like this:

HEX: The blessing IS the curse

Sweet Northern Friend ©Kelly Tingle Kazmierski

THE MAN BY THE RIVER

RICK FOWLER

Every small town with a river running through it has one. The guy, the man, the go to person when a change of lure (size and color) or live bait is needed; local anglers usually know him by his first name only Lou, Jim, Vern or by a nick name Crazy Bob, Tom the Trout Man. Last names don't matter much on the river. Honesty and a handshake do!

I first noticed him when I was twelve-years-old. He was dressed in well-worn jeans, a faded madras shirt and black high-top converse sneakers. On his head he had on a Tigers cap that seemed to crunch down on the brown curls spilling around his forehead and ears. He was old! But then again, to a twelve-year-old, even twenty something people were old.

Two or three times a week during this summer with the man by the river I would make my way to the banks on my banana seat Schwinn with a Zebco rod and reel, a can of night crawlers and a small metal tackle tote filled with sinkers, extra hooks and a plethora of rusty metal lures confiscated from my dad's thirteen compartment, plastic tackle box. The man would always be there it seemed. He would glance at me, give a shrug, nod his head and then continue casting. One day after he had landed a few nice trout and I had nothing to show for my efforts, I approached him.

"Um mister, don't mean to bother you, but I was just wondering what you were catching those trout with?" When he turned to answer I noticed he wasn't that old, not like thirty or forty anyway. He still wore the same jeans, the baseball cap, and the sneakers but the grin he gave me betrayed his youthfulness. "They are a little hungry today so I've been feeding them up a nice breakfast of spawn. Seems to work!" And that was it. No other conversation, no other tips, no other words of encouragement.

With that done, I then worked my way up and down the river looking for a honey-hole where my recipe of night crawler on a hook might be gulped. I left my makeshift tackle box by my bike and went exploring. When I returned, the man by the river was gone. There was however, a small glass container lying by the kickstand. Inside the tiny baby food jar there were two fresh spawn sacks inside cooled by a few ice cubes.

I saw the man by the river a few more times that summer. However, I never talked to him again. I was too shy to say thanks for his kindness, believing that if it hadn't been him who had left the spawn I would be totally embarrassed. He would acknowledge my presence every time I would pass near him, but few words were shared.

Things lead to things as they do and my treks to the river became fewer and fewer. School, sports, girls, college, career and marriage often occupied more and more of my fishing time. Over the next few decades fishing at least by the river was not as much of a priority as it used to be. It was, in fact, more than 50 years later, when a chance visit to a local bait shop offered me a glimpse of the now, seventy plus man by the river. The hair was still curly, but shorter and whiter now. We engaged in small talk. Apparently he had been working in various bait shops in the area "for the past thirty years" off and on to supplement his income. "Landscape work only lasts for a few months every year. Then I would get laid off. Since I love fishing and know a lot about the local waters I just seemed to be a good fit for this type of work. Now that I'm retired I can help more people who like to fish."

Was that a twinkle in his as he finished his sentence? Was there a hint of recognition on his part too? "So, a serving of spawn would be the appropriate breakfast for trout today?" I ask.

"Yep can't go wrong with spawn all day long, I always say."

I offered my hand to the man by the river and looked into his eyes as I said, "Thank you for helping me!" His grip was strong. His calloused hands had moved a lot of dirt over the years and his fingers had released thousands of fish from the hook. Now they were getting my accolades for his kind words and actions from so many years ago.

It didn't seem right that I should delve into the past to ask if he might remember that moment in time on the river. The handshake had been enough.

Thanks also to every Lou, Jim, Vern, Crazy Bob, Tom the Trout Man and other 'men by the river'. Your unselfish acts towards anglers are appreciated.

TOGETHER
(Lake Michigan dune, 2019)

JAN SHOEMAKER

My love,
thunder winds down
to the rumble of surf,
gale to the breath
of a browsing doe,
and the Fundy tide
to a tidal pool
stirred by the
antics of snails.
For years
we have walked
this path,
through ferns
and stippled light,
and climbed this slope
of glacial till
overlooking the beach.

Today we
felt a tremor
in the ledge
beneath our feet
prophesying the
sloughing bluff
that will carry us
back to the sea.

JULY 4

PHILLIP STERLING

Holiday or not, our
Eurasian daylilies celebrate,
rocketing orange noise

beneath the hummingbird
feeder, itself an envy
of bee balm, our native

Oswego tea. (One way,
at least, of looking at it.)
Tonight the moon will wax

with joy, and the fireflies
rise to dusk like lips
at the throat of the divine.

JULY IS TO RELATIVE AS SAILOR IS TO FAMILY

PHILLIP STERLING

The next day we track
the path of groundwater

from its source on the farm
to the shore of a vast lake

where a frigate—
or maybe a freighter

laden with ore—lengthens
its applause of wind's

tidy waves. For hours
its progress defines horizon,

declines any cause for
argument (its proper

heading, our distance
from it, the commerce

and metaphor of ballast)
—and then sky

alone. We'd met no one
on the journey. No god

waylaid us. And now
the few clouds at our disposal

ignore our presence. *Here*
the world's a given place,

save for us. We confer,
attribute. We acquiesce

and find our way back
by circumnavigation.

OCTOBER SPEAKS OF DIGNITY

PHILLIP STERLING

It's like a punky stump
festooned with orange fungi

no longer resentful
of the woodcutter

A RELIGIOUS EXPERIENCE

JOHN LENNON

There's something holy about
Sound passing through forest air
On solitary summer nights.

The gospels of lakes
Have saved more souls
Than waters have taken.

Psalms sung by streams
And hymnals of birds
Leave no heart untouched.

So spare me your prayers,
I will take the trees.
This cedar cathedral
Is the religion I need.

ELK RAPIDS SUNSET

SHELLEY SMITHSON

Orange sherbet drapes across the western sky
Cascading over the sleepy crocodile, Old Mission Peninsula.
Purples and hues of pink leak from the etched line of orange,
Melting the cells between my ribs so that with each breath
I seem to yearn to merge with that sunset.
I want to wrap myself in that sunset and walk back home silently.
Over the pine needled path around the library hill,
Smelling the pine scent as it dilates my bronchioles.
And I keep breathing in the colors, the smells,
Walking across the library bridge, I turn again
To see the glow of the orb of the sun,
Now clearer in the panorama before me
As it gently lowers itself behind the Old Mission Hills,
Seven miles yonder across Grand Traverse Bay, but close enough to touch.
Leaving me standing there, with the breeze gushing through the canopy of trees,
And the Grand Traverse Bay waves singing
In the shadows of the burning horizon.
I let the wind whip through my hair as
I thank the sunset for bidding me goodnight.

DIVIDEND ENOUGH

GLEN YOUNG

I knew one old high school teacher who never
believed in the honesty of rivers or ponds,
but rather what he said were truer constants,
angles and cycles, those geometries of the past,
worn parallels of evaluation. He was unaware
how the pass-fail of an afternoon kneeling in some
cathedral of low hanging limbs over moving water
is dividend enough, the better livelihood earned
out of doors in the company of forest or high bank,
any chevron of geese overhead, or the scissored
gill plate of brook trout the more perfect lines.

PORCH POEM

TAYLOR TUCKER

In the early months, a craggy island crouched
in frigid grey waters
waiting.
And its white stucco cottage
hunched in heavy snowbanks,
anticipating.

And then, as with the turning tide:

the clouds dissipated,
the sun lit a bright azure sky.
Tender, hungry skin
came out into the light
ready to metamorphose
to leather.

That day, on the little side porch, scraped and repainted,
she sat in the sun a long time—
the first sun in a long time, even though it was April;
the sun was still a stranger, stranger still
to behave in such a way.

She'd been building fires
to keep warm, dwindling the oak supply
from the great storm summers before.
She would not need the fireplace now.
Where have you been? she asked the sun with a smile.
I've been expecting you.

And so she sat on the top step in the quiet
yellow and green and blue,
book in hand,
with her dog's muddy black paws
hanging over the edge

while before them shone the northern water
they'd known their whole lives
finally come out in young light.

89 STEPS

RICK FOWLER

With a starry cloak above me I moved toward the lull of lapping waves and the dock that seemed to be waiting for me. After many years this ritual at our small Upper Peninsula lake front cabin was non-descript for my family. Much like leaving for work every morning at a specified time, my journey to the end of the dock was a given with each night's stay at the cabin.

This Saturday evening, as the early October winds began picking up, I wondered how much mileage the cedar dock sections had borne under my footsteps. How many trips had I made to the end? How many star-lit nights had I witnessed 100 feet out on the water? How many drops of rain had pelted me into submission? How many gusts had nearly toppled me into the turbulent waters? How many evenings had I held my children's hands as they walked with me cautiously, to view the aura of an August meteor shower? How many times had my wife and I ventured onto these sections to contemplate our place in the world, our love, and our children? How many fish had I caught, landed, admired and released back into the cool waters?

Over the course of twenty-five years, I have taken hundreds of treks. Eighty-nine steps out! Eighty-nine steps back!

Tonight, the weathered slabs creaked a bit as I started out. Armed with a dependable, but aging rod and reel, I flicked the switch on my headlamp and proceeded. The fourteenth step sparked a memory.

Were we ready for second home ownership? Could we afford it? With two young children, 3 and 1 should we try and afford it?

From the third section of dock that first summer, my daughter landed her first bluegill. We gently released it and I held her hand till we reached the shoreline. With a burst of energy, she raced to tell her mother. This defining moment confirmed our decision had been a good one.

Like a miner descending into the abyss of coal, my lamp illuminates the way as I move out further. At step thirty-three I pause, shut off my light and gaze upward.

As I remember there were millions of lights flickering in the sky on our third July at the cabin. Our entire family was on the dock looking skyward at the IMAX Theater of the heavens. Sue and I pointed out a few of the constellations: Ursa Major, Ursa Minor, the Seven Sisters. Suddenly we noticed movement to the north. The quickly moving object captured our attention for minutes before we realized what it was. A satellite, programmed by man for a journey unknown to us was rapidly orbiting our section of the universe. To two young children and their parents it was a marvel.

The winds are getting brisker as I make my way along. At step seventy-seven, the cone of light my lamp threw out fell upon the snakelike form of a deadhead that had occupied this space next to the dock for years.

It had been a night much like this. *The fishing had been slow at the end and, since I had had no luck, I decided to make a cast and let the crawler rigged hook settle on the bottom. I went back toward shore to see if I could finally remove the log firmly settled into the silty bottom. Gusts were causing some unbelievable wave action on this night wetting the cedar planks. My lesson in how slippery cedar can get when wet, happened suddenly. I approached the log and began to reach down ward. Just then another strong burst of wind flung me backwards a bit. I overcompensated and with stumbling feet careened into the water belly-flop style. None the worse for wear, I heaved myself back up, retrieved my fishing rod and made my way back into the cabin. To my amazement the entire family was sleeping, thus saving me a bit of an embarrassing moment.*

Step eighty-nine!

I had a special spoon on tonight's menu, a colorful red and white rapala. I unhooked it from the fourth eyelet, making sure there were no snags in the line, switched off the lamp and cast out into the jet-black waters. Slowly, methodically, I wind the line back onto the spool, and cast again. On the third, I feel tension.

One night in our tenth summer I had felt the same tension. Arriving at the cabin hours before, the winds had calmed. The lake was placid and splashed with a myriad of sunset colors. Outfitted with my ever-present rod and reel I baited the hook this night with a simple crawler and sinker combination and cast out to the South side where the reeds were elevated. Within seconds the creature struck and the line became taut as the tension increased. The last glimpse of light melted behind the western sky and soon I was encased in darkness. With no light, I couldn't tell what manner of species I had hooked. With a battle that would have pleased a saltwater fisherman, I managed to get my foe to the dock. It felt and had fought like a walleye, and in the obscure shadows I realized I was right. I put my catch into a creel, headed back to shore and burst into the cabin exclaiming, "Look at this monster!" Alas, again this night, everyone was sleeping. I weighed the fish in at four pounds and released him gently into the cool, wave less waters, secretly hoping to meet him again.

Tonight however, there would be no lunkers. The once brightly lit sky had given way to billowing clouds, and I noticed lightning in the distance.

A similar light show was also evident one evening last summer when Sue and I walked out hand in hand, with lawn chairs in the other and proceeded to prop ourselves down at the end of the dock. We marveled at the beauty of the evening sky, the approaching storm the rapid growth of our children, how thankful we were to have what we had, and relished in the decision we had made years earlier to purchase our cabin up north.

Tonight, as the soft pellets of rain begin to fall, I gather my gear and began to walk towards the dimly lit cabin eighty-nine steps away.

© TDIT

Flag Point ©Taylor Tucker

Wings of Wonder ©Kelly Tingle Kazmierski

REVISION

DEDA KAVANAGH

To walk in just the light
the moon lavishes,
to forfeit bright daylight,
to still be able to see
and prosper,
not to trip or be startled
in this obscure mist.
There is no knowing here
only asking, What is right?

What is left?
In the untextured distance
the only prowler
hoots her song,
her parliament tucked
and nuzzled
deep in some quaking aspen.
She knows I trespass here
sees me wondering
a mettlesome imposter,
caressing somber night.

STAG

ELLEN LORD

Autumn Equinox

chill of dawn heralds the fall

summer's final kiss

lingers on the vibrant trees

Eros appears in velvet.

A HAIKU TRILOGY FOR A MICHIGAN SUMMER

ELLEN LORD

I

Succulent July
Ripe cherries and rhubarb pie
Smack-red juicy smile

Hatchlings dart and dive
Nature's bounty ripening
Everywhere a song

Unfettered swallows
Flock flung far into the sky
Unsullied pure flight

II

Soft-mist morning
Delicate legs prance and pause
Twin fawns frolicking

To be astonished
Diving into cool silk
Northern sun kissed lake

Seductive summer
Lean, bronze, sinewy ripple
Wet undulation

III

Transient beauty
Lush blossoms reach for the sun
To covet, then mourn

Restless in August
Geese flock to the fields of grain
Southward bound again

Wild seasons of soul
Riotous and windswept
Landscape of the heart

Northern Lights ©Kelly Tingle Kazmierski

THE GIFT OF THE TIN BOX

NANCY RENKO

"If the stories are not told and the songs not sung, the land will die."
Wilson Hunter, Navajo Ranger, National Park Service

Neegoosis (Ojibwe word for son), remembered it well, for how could he forget that period of his childhood when so much was lost. He recounted the story truthfully and accurately as had been the custom among his people. He was the first member of his tribe to carry on the oral tradition of this event, but many more chroniclers would keep the narrative alive. The assigning of history to story tellers meant that each generation would carry the stories forward as certain as the waves followed one after another to the shore in their unending song of the sea. He stood tall and with a clear voice began the story of the gift.

"'Noos, (Ojibwe word for father), can we open the secret box now? We are almost there; soon we will see the waganawkezee, and we will be home.' "

He recounted how tribal ancestors had constructed the waganawkezee, a landmark called the crooked tree, by lashing a small pine to a stake in the water. In his mind's eye, he watched as the pine grew taller and taller, extending its trunk over the surface of the bay jutting out to mark the Odawa homeland which started in Harbor Springs, and stretched as far as the Straits of Mackinaw.

He continued the story, remembering each detail as he recalled it.

"The boy pestered, 'But Noos, the stranger said we could open it when we were home.' "

Negoosis momentarily flashed back to the birchbark canoe as it slithered through the pristine Michigan shoreline of L'Arbre Croche and he remembered the swishing sound it made followed by the soft rhythmic splash of the paddles slicing the mirrored surface of the Lake Michigan.

"The watercraft approached the village where we could see signs of life as other tribe members returned from their winter migrations and began to set up camp, gather food, and build cooking fires."

" 'It is good to return to the land of the setting sun, and yes, Neegoosis, we will be able to open the container soon. I bought it as a gift for the people, so it must be opened at a gathering of all the people. We can present it at the tribal council after we sleep tonight and fish in the morning.'"

" 'Tell me again what the white man said when he sold you the box, does it have magical powers?'"

" 'He told us not to open the package until we make our way back to our own country, remember little one? He said it contained something that will do us great good, a great good for the people.' "

" 'I've never seen a vessel such as this one, Noos. it is not made of clay like our pots, nor of quills like our quill boxes, nor of black ash like the baskets that grandmother makes. It shines like the sun, and it surely must be magic.' "

" 'It is made from tin, Neegoosis, that is a metal forged by the white men. It is beautiful but it's what's inside that interests me most.' "

"Noos kept the box secure as they unpacked the canoe and entered the birchbark wigwam ready to rest his tired limbs after a long journey."

The keeper of stories paused in the telling as he thought about his father, Noos, a kind but courageous man whose only passion was for the Odawa people. As his son, Negoosis, could only hope to live up to his father's legacy. He understood that keeping the oral tradition for the tribe was an important role and that this story especially would express a truth that each member of the tribe needed to know.

He began again, his memory strong like a wind that cuts through the trees, he noted:

"Daylight came too soon as Noos awoke and prepared for the tribal council. He felt proud of the gift he would present to the tribe. However, his anticipation could not compare with the excitement of Neegoosis, his son. As a child of nine winters. he was riddled with anticipation as he held the special box in his small hands, turning it round and round in wonderment. ' "

" 'I will remember this day,' said Neegoosis proudly. 'It will become one of the traditions of our people.' "

" 'It is your job to remember for the Ottawa nation, little one. You have a grave responsibility as a keeper of stories to hold our history and to pass it on to the next generation, and to the next keeper.' "

" 'Soon we shall see a great good contained in this gift, and the people will honor you for your generosity,' Negoosis .' "

" 'This honor is not for me, my son, it is rather for the noble Odawa people, who will grow to greatness as was intended by our ancestors.' "

Negoosis remembered: "As the sun rose high in the sky, scattering its rays across the calm water until it resembled a pile of shimmering gems, the father and son fished together, then began the long walk up the sand dunes to the place where the tribal council convened. It was a clearing on the other side of the dunes, which stood in the shelter of tall pines growing in a circle, a sacred symbol for the people."

He added: "When it came time for Noos to present his gift, the council members straightened their backs, standing tall to show their gratitude for such a fine present. The chief opened the shiny tin and was surprised to see that inside this box was another smaller box made from the same shiny material. He opened the second box only to see a third box. Everyone in the circle became more and more curious crowding closer as another box was opened until, finally there remained only the smallest box which was about one inch long. "

" 'Surely, this must be something very powerful in such a tiny package,' Noos commented. 'It will bring a great good to the people.' "

The Keeper explained further: "When the last tin was finally opened, there was great disappointment amongst those present, as they found only a few scraps of moldy particles. Noos was especially crestfallen that his gift, purchased from the profits of furs he traded, was worthless. With his best warrior posture, he walked from the tribal council back to his lodge with a hole in his heart. The chief kept the box, in case its mystery would be later revealed to them. He kept it in his wigwam and waited to see if the moldy particles would produce any results."

With a wash of emotion Negoosis told the sad truth. "Within a matter of days, the tribe realized the power of the gift as members of each lodge fell ill with fever, chills, pustular rash and scabs. Even the medicine men were taken ill and died from the small-pox virus contained in the tin.

Entire families were wiped out from the disease, and the native population in L'Arbre Croche was completely decimated."

"My Father and I both fell ill early in the outbreak. Noos burned with fever, then spoke in a parched voice to me. You, my son, are young and strong. You will see many more sunrises. As a keeper of tradition, you must mark this day, young warrior, and remember it always.' "

Negoosis related how he had wept softly but promised his father even while moaning through his suffering, "I will live in your footsteps, always doing good for our people."

In his writings, Chief Andrew J. Blackbird, recounted the oral history of this horrific event in a book entitled, *A History of the Ottawa and Chippewa Indians in Michigan*. The history includes an account of the outbreak of a small-pox epidemic during the height of the French and Indian wars, about 1757. It was believed that the box was purchased from a supporter of the British who plotted to wipe out the Native Americans who were allies of the French. According to Blackbird's account, the virus was transferred from a box that was brought from Montreal to Northern Michigan.

Tragically, an act of war resulted in genocide which altered history. The numbers of indigenous people in Northern Michigan were forever decreased, but the story of the tin box was kept alive through oral tradition until Chief Blackbird recorded it as written history.

Today, when driving the scenic road along M-119 through the tunnel of trees, one can see burial mounds near the historic Odawa settlement of Cross Village. It has been said that the Ottawa people were buried in graves that stacked four to five bodies, the victims of a small-pox epidemic spread through the gift of the tin box.

Sunrise Brockway Mountain ©Melissa Seitz

RELIQUARY

GREG RAPPLEYE

Until the water comes sweet
the well flows a slurried clay—
for three days, an acre of blue-gray marl
swamps the copper well-head.
I'm kneeling at the mire's soggy edge
with mollusk shells, with a Jesus bug
plucked from the creek,
with pine needles and oak leaves
and hard little acorns fallen from trees
atop the hill. Da's dream
is to pipe what good water comes
to an orange-painted shack
he's building; to stir up dark root beer,
to sell cheeseburgers and chili dogs
and greasy chips all summer
to tourists ferrying out to the island.
My dream? To press these shells,
this dead shiner, my leaves and seed cones
to the wet clay, sure these will harden
into fossils I might varnish, number
and glue into a cedar box;
to scrawl pig latin names for each,
and amaze the many children I'll have
in forty years or-so. Who could have guessed
that when the rain came in torrents
my relics would wash away,
that the good water would last but twenty years
until a leach of rancid fry grease spoiled it,
and that through those cold decades
the madness that tumbled boulders against the pines,
that gouged and surged across the frozen blue lakes
and down the Sturgeon every damned night
would mold a boy's heart into stone?

IN A DREAM, MY FATHER DECIDES TO GO ICE FISHING

GREG RAPPLEYE

Da calls collect from Hell. Says, spud a hole
through the candy-ass ice. Hammer our sign,
blood red, above the shanty door.
He's not here for crappies. Not come for bluegills,
big as your useless hands. He's trolled this trench
on squalid summer nights, has milted the eggs
and sunk a battered Nash to build a reef;
has nursed these schools from glow-worm sprats
and is going deep again—after bull huss and viperfish,
after alligator gar, after eelpouts and snakeheads,
all gilling across the silt of our secret spot;
their needle-teeth, their banjaxed eyes and grisly heads,
their hellish Miltonic fins. Whatever we hook
we'll toss, gasping onto lake-ice, scattered out between
the shanty and the sled. So cold they'll be, frozen
before they recall open water, as we smoke and shudder
and drink. And which of us, my prodigal, will
walk out under the wolf moon and blistering stars
tally the haul, and have a final sip as the other
drifts away? Who'll rise before dawn, stack the sled
with carcasses, and leaving the last to dream alone,
drag our dead back to the distant piney shore?

SEARCHING FOR SUNLIGHT

JOHN LENNON

I parked my car,
Strapped my snowshoes,
Followed trail markers,
Then deer tracks,
Then rabbit prints,
And then hollow knocks
Of pileated delight,
And as I reached the peak,
Dormant lakes and cataract skies
Gave way to sunbeams:
Proof winter will not last.
Hope will blossom
Like roses in garden,
Tall grass on dunes,
Lilies in stream,
And our stars into view.

GRAND TRAVERSE IN WHITE

EDD TURY

Frozen out to Northport
first time in years they say.
We could walk from Antrim Creek to Omena
if we had enough time and young bodies.

Now it's enough to skitter out to the edge
where the frozen mounds of last month's waves
mark the beginning of deep water
so silent under the bright white ice.

How small is this beautiful bay
given the boundless universe
and how smaller yet are we
standing out in this frozen expanse.

In this holy spot together for the first time in our lives
we pray to gods that exist only in private dreams.
This is a once in a lifetime hike
across hard water.

On the other side is darkness.

ROCKER

SKIP RENKER

On this summer porch next to a river,
My arms resting over its arms, old woven
Wicker coming undone around the legs,
This rocker still smells faintly of smoke
Mingled with my mother's perfume.

I've inherited its rhythms, remembering
How she settled in at last after cooking
And laundry for my father and nine children,
After the hurrying, the scolding, the caressing
Away of countless hurts. She rocks and smokes,

Looks out through the living room window at dark
Maples, Little Traverse Bay in the far distance.
She raises that evening cigarette to her lips
In a slow graceful gesture, draws the smoke deep,
Tilts her head back and blows out a long plume.

She lived twenty-five years after she quit,
But even as the rhythm of her life slowed
Toward a full stop, and the doctors limited her
To half a glass of evening wine, she still
Knew how to savor, savor each sip.

Treasure Island ©Taylor Tucker

I MIGHT RIDE OFF

SKIP RENKER

Into the sunset over the lake
with a stranger, a newly hired nurse's aide
on evening duty, or an unfamiliar
custodian sweeping the hospice hallway
who hears what might be a death rattle,
peers in through my half-open door,

though the stranger could just as easily
be a portable machine, heart monitor with
an interrupted hum, or an oxygen pump
giving out. If these machines roll
with me then, toward the fiery
horizon, I'll touch them with extended
fingers, as I would my human relatives,
try to respect them for what they are
and were, useful companions,

but of course I'd prefer the company
of my wife, children, grandchildren,
my dog and the sunset-red underwings
of gulls, or even a horse from one of my
childhood comic books or television shows,
Trigger, Champion, Silver, though by then

I may well be tired of saddling up,
ready at last to ride easy, let
the western wind have my back.

DECEMBER 23, NORTHERN MICHIGAN

CJ GIROUX

Michigan winter has become Michigan water—
rain falls and falls
as in a Hemingway novel
Bearing bags of bulbs
clearanced at the dollar store,
I pull down the decomposing leaves
banking the cabin's foundation
to create cushions for dwarf tulip, purple
hyacinth, oversized allium.
I unwrap their outer skins like tissue paper,
place tips toward grey sky
before blanketing the future
with wet loam.

Awaiting messiahs who will make mudpacks
on the Sabbath, send the blind to bathe
in the waters of Siloam,
I find neither revelations nor healing,
just the chill of rain, the glare of neighbors
who refuse eye contact, live behind glass.
For the moment, the wet soil feels like war paint
coating fingers, cuffs, cheek,
and the damp weather a second skin.
Working faster, wanting warmth,
I fell the last stalks of anise hyssop
and think of funeral sprays as I spread
this blue fortune over the ground,.
I want epiphanies, but all I have are dreams
of Leelanau springs
and Charlevoix summers:
the return of cherry blossoms,
the thrum of bees, the gift of warm air
marked with licorice and lavender.

MUD SEASON

EDY STOUGHTON

Soggy, gloomy, dreary
Winter's snowy blanket, covering all in softness, hiding flaws
is melting.
We are left with mud.
Sloshy, oozy,
Sticking to pants legs, shoes and the dog's paws
"Does he really need to go out?"
His favorite ball is buried under the ooze
I'm weary of dealing with muddy floors.

Somber tones of brown—a monochrome landscape
No billowy clouds or brilliant bursts of sun,
The sky a leaden sheet of thick, pale gray
A sense of waiting, of suspended animation.

No more drama of winter snowstorms
No more shrieking winds, no blinding snow
No more watching the inexorable progress of the storm,
fire blazing.
Red wine and a good book
No excitement.

No sounds of pounding waves
The ice-trapped lake is still.
No sounds of anything
Total absence of noise and movement
A silent, muted world

The trees stand motionless as the fog rolls in
Shrouding them, leaving only shadowy forms.
I am alone and solitary in a featureless world of uniform grayness.
Days are monotonous, cheerless, sullen
"Fog again?"
"How long since we've seen the sun?"

Yet there is a strange sort of beauty in this somber world
Surrounded by fog-softened edges and hushed soundlessness I move more slowly and take time to contemplate.
There is space to read a good book, create a painting, write in a journal.
In the isolation, I am forced to connect with my own thoughts and dreams.
It drives me into myself
I stare moodily out the window
Our fox lopes down the dune
His handsome russet coat blending with the sepia-toned browns and grays around him.

There is quiet loveliness in the muted colors
Subdued shades and soft hues,
Nature's more subtle, less showy side
Gloomy, sloshy, drippy, yes
Unrelentingly monotonous
But also, a respite
A time of renewal for this world and for me.
I'm still ready for the sun to return.

EXPOSURE

MELISSA SEITZ

Outside my window,
the glass as cold as death,
a winter storm suffocates
the morning sky,
removes the horizon's edges
as I search for light.

In the semi-darkness,
I reach for the switch
on my late father's amber lamp.
Click—blurred light
permeates the room as if
everything floats under water.

Outside wind chimes rattle disjointed songs of warning.
A fox trots across the frozen lake, turns, and
glances at me as I watch his search for prey.
My brain's hippocampus
recalls bursts of blinding light
and fiery sunrises of days past.

Scrolling backwards through my camera's memory card,
light and dark images morph
into one long slide show
of months of sunrise photos.
Slipping on my coat, my camera strap over my head,
I open the door.

I step outside and walk towards the light,
sinking into fresh snow, watching cardinals
flying frantically between bird feeders,
their blood red and pale-brown feathers
flashing through pine trees
reminding me to provide their daily sustenance.

Stopping where shoreline ice creates fractured shelves,
I plant my boots in deep pockets of snow,
remove the lens cap from my camera,
and focus on the faintest hint of a sunrise edging into view.
Once again, I capture the ephemeral glow of the morning light.

GUARDIANS OF THE NORTHERN LAKES

AMY ZARANEK

The cricket in the corner chirps as the coffee percolates. Acorns hit the roof like artillery. A mourning dove laments from the row of trees that used to be the property line.

The air is still, the earth shrouded by the late summer humidity combined with smoky remnants of the western states' wildfires. Tall pines stretch upward in the grey light of morning. Treetops barely stand out against the haze. Any semblance of a breeze striates the water's glassy surface, where ripples look like raindrops.

I look out at the lake and see two loons surface just past the dock. One of them lets out a call. Its mourning timber echoes through the earliness. The loons flap their wings to rid their feathers of water, sending sprays of droplets reflecting into the lake's surface: a mirrored suspension between earth and sky.

I turn back to the stove, where I was cooking breakfast before I saw the loons. Then I catch myself. I used to drop what I was doing and rush to the window, usually grabbing binoculars to look at the loons more closely. I used to fully experience them.

What happened? Had I become so accustomed – so jaded – to seeing the legend play out in my own watery front yard that it had become dismissible?

In fourth grade, every child in Michigan's public schools learns the state's history. My teacher proudly imparted the facts upon us. This is where we are from. This is our home. Michigan was the twenty-sixth state admitted to the Union, and it stayed in the Union in the 1860s, when Detroit became a key destination on the Underground Railroad. The nicknames: Great Lakes State, the Mitten. The industries: automobiles, logging, mining, agriculture. The Latin word above the man on the state flag: *Tuebor.* We will defend.

In addition to fourth-grade state facts, we learned legends of the Native tribes who were here long before any of my ancestors. The Three Nations – Algonquin, Chippewa, and Potawatomi – called the state home in a peaceful coalition known as the Council of Three Fires. In a loose way, my classmates and I learned tribal tales of the formation of the world and pre-geologic explanations for the state's terrain.

The one I remembered most was of the creation of loons.

An old woman lived on a lake, deep in the north woods. She lived alone, but each day, was visited by her two grandsons. She taught them lessons that the woods imparted upon her over her long life: how to find a trail, how to forage for food, how to live for the art of survival where the woods met the water. From her, the boys learned to paddle a canoe and catch fish. At night, they would build a fire, cook their fish, and listen as she told them stories of their shared past.

She wore a black and white shawl and a necklace of bone. The firelight cast a red glow into her eyes. Shadows danced upon her shawl, a reflection of the night sky across her back and shoulders. By the fire in the darkness, she exuded an elderly beauty comprised of all she had seen and done, and her voice became otherworldly.

The boys grew to be strong and capable men. They could paddle canoes swiftly and navigate rapids with ease. They knew the best trails to trap food and find berries. They built their homes on the lakeshore near their grandmother's hut, and never forgot the lessons she taught them.

The grandmother, already an old woman, seemed indestructible – almost immortal – in the boys' youth. But as time passed, she began to show signs of her age: she stooped at the waist and adopted a shuffling walk. She was slow and clumsy on land, but her canoe still glided across the water with ease.

One morning, she walked to the water's edge as she always did to retrieve her canoe. She shuffled along the smooth, rocky beach. She shuffled past the canoe, and shuffled into the water. She gained strength and grace with each step deeper. A heavy mist closed in on the lake. Her otherworldly voice echoed through the ether, somewhere between wailing and laughter. When it cleared, she was gone.

A formerly-unseen bird was in her place. It was black and white, with a white necklace and the night sky splashed across its back and shoulders. Its red eyes reflected the light of a thousand fires. When it let out a call, it was a familiar wailing laughter that the boys heard since childhood. They knew that this new bird would continue to guide them, just as the old woman guided them through the days of their youth.

At least, that is how I remembered the story. I was met with a reality check when I recently revisited the tale in the way it was retold in my fourth-grade classroom. In it, the grandchildren – a boy and a girl – were warned not to take the boat past the drop-off at the edge of the bay where their grandmother lived. As they paddled out, their journey was obscured by fog, and they lost their way. They drifted past the drop-off. Their grandmother heard their cries from shore and rushed into the water, waving her arms and wailing in an attempt to locate them. When the children saw a strange new bird fly overhead, they knew their grandmother, their guardian, transformed into something to save them. She guided them home to safety.

I like my own recollection better. I like the independence my misconception affords, both for myself and for the characters. My imagination shaped them to be more congruent with my own values. Liberty in legends retold is more aligned with the oral storytelling tradition anyway; more so than revisiting a children's book fifteen years later and taking it word for word. There is value in the past, but also in what is made of the past–my own perception in the present. It can be hard to see clearly without the lens of time framing my perspective.

The northern Michigan summer after my first year of college, my aunt Gail sat near me on the dock. The wooden slats pressed into our legs, and our toes dangled into the crisp, clear lake. Her grandsons splashed in the water beneath us. Up the hill, my dad and his brother, Pierre, worked on home improvement projects.

My immediate family made frequent trips to the lake from our lives downstate; but my uncle Pierre and Aunt Gail didn't spend much time up north during my childhood. I don't remember them coming up a single time before I was in high school. But when I was older, Uncle Pierre and Aunt Gail visited the north more often with their grandsons. At first, they came up on the weekends when my family was there, then they used the house more on their own time, too. They were always gracious guests, using their trips to the north to teach their grandsons the value of gratitude and personal pride. Through their visits, I grew much closer with Uncle Pierre and Aunt Gail than I was in the past.

A loon surfaced a hundred yards out from the dock where Aunt Gail and I sat. He rose from his dive for fish at the drop-off, where the lake floor becomes a sandbar so clear that I can see every twig on the bottom. I spotted the loon immediately. When you're accustomed to looking at nothing, anything becomes easily noticeable.

As a child, I memorized the rises and falls in the lake floor from studying the aerial map that hung above the couch. Jeweled blue designated plunging depths. A pale, thin green meant shallowness that could ground a boat in a span of mere feet. The wooded banks gave the water the shape of a dog from the north or a rabbit from the south, and the island looked like its eye. An elk skull now hangs where the map once was, but its imprint on my brain allows me to see the depths designated by watercolor even on cloudy days.

The loon let out its distinct call, haunting amidst the August sunshine.

"Do you hear the elk?" Aunt Gail asked excitedly. "You can hear the elk bugling!"

I wanted to tell her no, it's a loon, it's right there, you can see it. It's too early for elk, it's still summer. They're not rutting yet. It's not an elk. It's a loon. Look.

It was something so clear to me, from my days in the north, that it was hard for me to believe that someone could mistake one for the other. To me, it was as if someone mistook my large dog for a lizard. I couldn't believe that she didn't see the loon right in front of us. It made its presence known. It gave itself up to be seen.

But it didn't matter. Correcting her would have made me sound self-righteous and unwelcoming. She hadn't spent the time here that I had. Neither she nor my uncle Pierre spent the weeks of summer and winter here that I did throughout my childhood. Neither of them grew up here.

"There's a loon, too," I said instead, pointing out its black head, regal like a knight. I just assumed that she would have known. Up until that moment, I took it for granted that I did.

That night, after we ate dinner and the sun set late, I took Uncle Pierre and Aunt Gail's grandsons on a night hike in the woods. The boys grew up in the city, as had I, and though they had begun to spend time away from urbanization, they weren't far enough removed from it to feel comfortable in the wild. During the day, they were happy in the woods. They laughed and explored, eager to experience new things.

But the woods were a different world in the dark. The shadows cast by the moon made the trees seem ominous. Their branches stretched above like skeletal arms silhouetted against blackness. Any breeze made leaves quake and boughs creak and any fallen limbs squeak like ancient bones. My dad frequently took me on night hikes as a child. Then, if I tried to look at everything, to turn around and glance behind me, my fear exponentially compounded. I could not take it all in. That was the scariest part.

Though I was afraid at first, I learned to accept my surroundings. Darkness is a part of light–something I still remind myself within the zippered security of my tent. Just because things aren't seen doesn't mean they aren't there, but it also doesn't mean that they are. Sometimes it takes a shift of focus to change an experience.

I wanted Uncle Pierre's grandsons to have a similar experience in the woods at night. I wanted them to feel comfortable there. Neither of the boys had yet reached their teenage years. They were young and jumpy, fearful in their youth of things unseen. Uncle Pierre and my dad came along with us. We entered the woods, and felt the trees close in around us as we ventured farther down the trail.

"Was that a wolf?" the boys whispered at the call of a loon.

"No, there are no wolves here," I told them.

Moments later, "was that a bear?" It was Uncle Pierre rustling a branch behind the boys. I almost told him to stop, but I knew his heart was in the right place. It was a well-intentioned prank. He was always quick with a joke, and even quicker with a laugh that I inherited, a laugh that sounded like he'd never heard anything funnier in his life–air escaping his lungs all at once.

"That was your papa," I told the boys. They looked around, found him in the dark, and laughed. They began to feel at-ease. I showed them constellations and shared legends about the Big and Little Dippers and Cygnus, the swan, the summer cross. I told them about the way the night sky changes in winter, and how people below the equator see an entirely different sky than we do in the north.

Then we all formed a circle. Time to learn about echolocation. I had one boy–the bat–stand in the middle, eyes closed, as I chose his brother to be my accomplice–the bug.

"Okay, if you're in the middle, you're the bat," I said. "Try to find the bug somewhere on the outside. You can only communicate with chirps.

Ready? Go!"

Both brothers began to chirp back and forth. The brother in the middle struggled to locate the source of the responding chirp. He held his arms in front of him as he walked a sweeping, erratic pattern around the circle we formed. Soon, though, he narrowed down his search. He was able to pinpoint his prey, his bug-brother, and grabbed hold of him. The young brothers peeled into a fit of giggles. In their moment of childhood glee, my mind turned to wondering. Of our group that night, I was the only one of my generation, the only person not paired with a sibling. I was the only woman in the woods.

I looked at the other set of brothers through the darkness: my dad and my uncle. Their fifteen-year age gap was too large to have played such games together in their childhood. Were they living vicariously through the boys, two generations down the line? What memories did they have that could compare to this one? Were they reflecting too, or was this an entirely new memory, fully experienced in the moment and lived for its own value?

I pulled myself from my generational reflection and fished a stash of wintergreen mints from my pocket. The mints emit light when they're bitten, and light is much more visible at night. It's an effect called triboluminescence, and stems from crushed molecules disrupting the electrons in their atomic fields. These electrons interact with nitrogen, which vibrates and emits an ultraviolet light, mixed with small amounts of visible light. But I didn't know that at the time. I only knew that if you chew a wintergreen mint at night, you can see your mouth spark in the darkness. We all laughed as we held lightning in our mouths.

Then I showed them how to use peripheral vision to look at things at night. It was a trick guaranteed to spook the boys. They each partnered up with one of the men and stood across from each other. I told them to look directly at their partner's head, just to stare right at it. Seconds later, I heard their shifting and sounds of unsettlement. The space where their partner's head had been was replaced by nighttime. Looking for too long made something they knew to be there be gone. I told them to try again, but to look over their partner's shoulder instead. This time, everyone's head stayed intact, because it was in their peripheral vision. Their central vision was focused elsewhere, so their peripheral vision could pick up the object they wanted to see.

If you look directly at things, they disappear.

Three years later, my uncle Pierre felt bloated after Thanksgiving and Christmas. He blamed the feeling on the feasts. He wrote it off until a few more weeks went by and he couldn't ignore it anymore. After the New Year, he went to the doctor. He was diagnosed with stage four pancreatic cancer on January 12, 2017.

He, with the help of Aunt Gail, made the choice to undergo chemotherapy, despite the slim odds and advanced nature of his disease. In the following weeks, he stayed in, aside from his treatments. He developed jaundice and contracted hiccups that lasted for days on end. I was home from Colorado, in between seasonal ranch jobs for the winter, so I was able to visit.

On my first visit, Uncle Pierre was in much better health than I expected him to be. He was sick, of course, but not far removed from the man playing jokes on our night hike, the man who played pinball with me as a child, the man who took me to a hot air balloon show as a toddler. He smiled and joked, and though walking on his own was difficult, he could still do it. Despite his dismal diagnosis, I held out hope. Miracles happen every day. Ask and you shall receive. I prayed for a miracle.

One week later, I visited again. During the week in between my visits, I hired on to a ranch in southern Colorado. I was set to start in a month. Uncle Pierre shared my love of the West and of the desert, and I was excited to tell him about where I'd be going next. When I arrived at his house, I realized that the tone of this visit would be much different than the first. If things had been better than expected on my first visit, this time, they were worse. Uncle Pierre's health declined rapidly in the past week. He was unable to walk on his own, and despite his inability to eat or drink anything besides chocolate milk, he was much more bloated than the week before. He wore a neon yellow shirt that made his jeweled, jaundiced skin seem even more golden. His shirt and skin contrasted with the purple rubber wristbands our whole family wore: "No One Fights Alone!"

Uncle Pierre had a hard time staying awake for a full conversation. I had a hard time not crying. But I managed to tell him about the ranch I was going to, the cattle and bison they raised, their Nature Conservancy owners and National Park neighbor.

"It sounds amazing. I hope it turns out to be everything you hope it will be," he told me.

When it was time to leave, I hugged uncle Pierre and told him I loved him. Aunt Gail walked me to the door, where I hugged her and told her to let me know if she needed anything at all. We hugged again, tears welling up in both of our eyes as we looked at each other. As I stepped out the door, I heard Uncle Pierre call out that he loved me one more time.

"Love you too!" I called back through the door. I glanced back inside at where he sat, his back to me as he started to fall back asleep. I knew it would be the last time I'd see him. I stopped praying for a miracle, and started praying for peace.

Uncle Pierre died later that week, on March 22 – only ten weeks after his diagnosis.

The thought that ran through my mind constantly in those ten weeks was how glad I was that I was home during that time. I was so happy that I could spend what little time I could with my uncle, and that I was close to home instead of worrying from a ranch two thousand miles away, trying to buy plane tickets or make travel plans. I was right there to create my last few memories of him in person. My uncle Pierre and I were close, without a doubt. But we were not as close as I am with some of his brothers, and certainly not as close as I am with my dad. I just kept thinking, *What if it had been one of them?* Someday, it will be.

I went to Uncle Pierre's funeral with my truck loaded to move back to Colorado. After the funeral reception, when the rest of my family was going home to continue the grieving process with their loved ones, I was getting in my truck and driving to a ranch where I'd only been for an interview, to live with people I'd never met. I cried as I crossed state lines. What was I doing? This was my career, but did it have to be so far away from the people I love? Who would be next, and would I be there for it?

With Uncle Pierre, something not seen caused something fully unforeseen. It was sheer coincidence that I was home that winter, that we were able to spend his last holiday season together. And I realized, I didn't want to be around only in the event of death. I wanted to be around to make memories with my entire family, like that night in the woods with my dad and Uncle Pierre and his grandsons. I wanted them to be a constant in my life, instead of dropping in for a week or a month here and there when the grazing season ended, or when we moved livestock to a lower elevation for the winter and I had time off. I wanted to see my family more often. I wanted them in the living part of my life.

Even though I was leaving, I knew I would no longer take it for granted that they'd be there when I got back. I crossed the Colorado state line knowing that when the season ended, I'd be going home to Michigan.

Misty nymphs dance across the water's surface on a morning that makes me believe in ghosts. Their arms drift wispily upward to greet the sun in gold – the dawn that will be their death, as they're burned off to reveal the flat sheet of liquid above the depths below.

I navigate my kayak toward the island. My freezing fingers curl around my paddle as water trickles from the blades.

Duck wings whistle overhead as they start to fly south. Their departure seems premature, but they must feel the same chill that I do this morning. I track them through the sky, above the powerlines strung across the Narrows, where abandoned lures from phantom fishermen hang like shoes on a wire.

A loon appears in a gap in the mist. Close. We stare at each other. I don't move. The first rule of wildlife observation is to keep your distance – for your own safety and for their sense of security. If you make an animal move, you're too close. *I will never disturb you,* I think to him. I've been on the island in the winter, when the loons leave the lake. But I'll never walk on their island when they're nesting. I'll never pull my kayak ashore and claim dominion over the land protected for them. I will not desecrate its wildness.

The loon cuts a line in the water directly in front of my kayak. He's close enough now that I can see the spots speckled and splattered across his wings and back. I can see the wide white necklace he wears on his proud neck. I can see the surprising fire in his red eyes.

Past my kayak, he circles once, a tight turn in still water. Rings of ripples begin beneath his body. He keeps his red eyes on me through the circle. I have never seen a loon act this way. Was it out of confusion or gratitude, or something wilder? A message is imparted, a deeper connection forms from the interaction. I fully experience it for what it is. The ripples spread toward me. He swims on.

This flat water is faster now that the sun has risen. The mist has burned off, freeing my kayak from its humid arms. But still it lurks in pockets of shadow. My own shadow shows the slice of my paddle, the lean and pull. I squint against the harsh reflection off the lake. The sun and my motion work together to warm me within the white down feathers peeking out among black like the spray of speckles on a loon's back. I paddle home.

Winning poetry and prose from The 17th Annual Young Writers Juried Exposition Petoskey, Michigan

The Crooked Tree Arts Center and Petoskey News-Review 17th Annual Young Writers Juried Exposition is supported in part by the Bob Schulze Fund for Creative Writing at the Petoskey-Harbor Springs Area Community Foundation, McLean & Eakin Booksellers and Walloon Writers Review.

MASTERPIECE

BRIELLE BURRIS

My brush glides across the paper. Painting steams of yellow and mint. Sounds of brush strokes mix with the chirping birds outside the window. My brush taps leaving dots of spring upon the masterpiece. Paint smears my hands but I don't mind. I paint.

First Place Poetry – Elementary School
Sheridan Elementary, Petoskey

A SLED DOG'S PLACE

EVA SHARAPOVA

I lifted my eyes from the forest, I was Shilah. Glancing upon my owner, Katie, I had been playing with my littermates, but, this was different. If I could make this work, I could finally earn my place in the pack. I am an Alaskan Malamute. These dogs are not often considered sled dogs, but Katie, wanted to prove them wrong, she could win the race without a single husky on her sled.

I turned back to the thick pine wood. My fur was neatly combed and groomed and around my neck, was a worn down collar that read "Swing Dog." Gently padding towards my pack, I lowered my head and wagged my tail, "sorry Shilah, we can't risk you being a leader or wheel dog. It might be too much for a pup like you." Katie said. I sat back on my haunches and watched Katie questioningly, when Katie didn't respond, I barked several times and leapt up on my hind paws trying to get her attention. My mother snapped at, revealing her teeth. Quickly, I backed down.

My sister, Leah was a swing dog as well. My other litter-sister, Eva, was a team dog as well as my littermates Ringo, Jinx and Lox. My mother and father were the lead dogs, Frost-pelt and Willows-breeze were the wheelers. Trotting over to the ice glazed lake, she sniffed the edge hoping to hear the sound of rushing water. Edging by the lake, I sniffed the air for the sweet scent of food and rushing water, my mother, Small-leap, was nosing her way towards me.

Like my mother, once I earned it, I would have a full name of my own. Father was leaping-grass and mother was small-leap. I felt my fur prick with excitement as Katie began to tie up the Wheelers, then the Team dogs. When it came my turn, I leapt up and stood still while Katie tied Leah's and my harness on. More behaved than the rest of us, mother and father took their place in the front. Katie bundled into the thick jacket she wore and took her place on the sled. "Come gee come haw, straight away!" manded for mother and father to lead the team straight. All of the sudden, they were running, it felt as though she was flying as their paws hammered against the snow. Then Katie uttered a command she hadn't heard before, "Whoa!" and they abruptly came to a stop. Other dogs lined up as well. Beneath them was a big black line that some humans must have painted on the ground.

My littermates paced excitedly, but, following my mother, I stood still and erect. "Ready & alright!" Katie's voice was followed by several others and all of the dogs stood still, ears pricked, I edged forward. The trail ahead turned into a sharp left turn. That was where Katie would give another command. There was a strange sound that a human made from a black object that smelled of fire, then, suddenly we were off. "HAW!" Katie's signal too move left was followed by each dog in my small pack… except mother. She slid and fell. Father immediately skidded to a stop and the few of us who couldn't stop, slid and fell on top of each other.

Katie raced out to kneel beside mother and check her over. Mother's leg had been bent the wrong way when she hit a tree, moving forward I sniffed the leg, mother snapped at me. Her eyes were glazed over with pain, Katie carefully lifted mother onto the sled, Father, following behind her, then as if Katie had planned this she took mothers collar off. I noticed a few of us.

Exchanging unsure looks, so I let out a sharp dominant bark. As Katie stroked mother's soft leather harness, she replaced it with mine, Katie took father out and put him in the Swing dog`s place where I had been. Taking me, Katie placed me in the Lead dog`s place and descended to the sled where, she muttered "Shilah, earn your place, if this won't work our sled packs gone, Ready & Alright!" I heaved forward and was suddenly aware of the weight behind me. The dogs ran with me though, she heard mother's loud barks from the sled, telling us in her own language to run harder than ever before. "Mush." Katie commanded, I could see the black outlines of the other sledders, frost was beginning to work its way through my fur, they disappeared around the ridge and as soon as Katie yelled "Gee!" the pack was right by another team, our team launched across the tundra beating the opponent by a whisker. Night was soon there, but Katie wouldn't think about pausing, if they stopped for too long, well... Small-Leap`s life was depending on this.

Quicker than before, she didn't hesitate to go through the night, small leap was her first sled dog and if she was gone. There was no hope. The dawn's light filtered through the tundra. They weren't far ahead of the rest of the competitors. And soon enough, a man not much older than Katie with his own pack of huskies was flanking us, not to be outdone, I sped up. Sure, they had two lead dogs, but they didn't have our pack! There was no way they would win. But sure enough, Katie had an idea, in a flash she had turned and yelling "gee!" we went through the woods, this was a shortcut, I could see the fury glittering on the man's face, there was the end. There was the gunshot. We had won! "Shilah! Shilah!" the words were happy when Katie said them and running to me, she unhooked the sledding harness, taking out a pocket knife, she crossed Shilah out and wrote: Swift-breeze. "Swift breeze." the words echoed out of her lips.

"Swift breeze." I thought, "I earned my name. I am finally a true pack dog!"

First Place Prose - Elementary School
St. Francis Xavier, Petoskey

POETRY IS

JOSIE ALEXANDER

Poetry is living, not surviving,
Being wild and free, not careful and hesitant,
Breaking the rules-and making your own,
Taking a leap, not a step.

Poetry is listening to an aged Vietnam vet talk about his journeys,
Playing a John Denver song in the car on a summer evening,
Going back to where I grew up and then seeing where I am now,
Looking into a wise person's eyes.

Poetry is when I see the mountains for the first time,
Taking a backcountry ski run in the deep snow,
Looking out at the never-ending mountain ranges,
And stopping to smell the pine trees.

Poetry is a deep breath before the rush of adrenaline,
Having the weight lifted off my shoulders,
For someone to say they are very proud of me and know they mean it,
To look into my father's eyes and see that he's complete
Just by the laughter of his children.

Poetry is seeing someone that I loved long ago and knowing that they're okay,
It's time after a heartbreak,
Accepting the truth,

Living on.

Poetry is the sound of the birds in the morning,
A snowy buffalo shaking off his fur coat,
The crickets being silenced by the thunder,
And the stalking eyes of an owl.

Poetry is the last goodbye,
The last mountain peak I see before I drive home,
The last breath of altitude,
And the last person I think about before I fall asleep.

Poetry is living, not surviving,
Being wild and free, not careful and hesitant,
Breaking the rules-and making your own,
Taking a leap, not a step.

First Place Poetry – Middle School
Boyne Falls Middle School, Boyne Falls

THE TRAIN

AUDREY GIETZEN

Finally, we heard the deafening scream of metal against metal and the trumpeting roar of the train's horn. I looked up at my father. We knew it was time. He squeezed my shoulder.

"Everything will be alright, son."

I knew it wasn't alright. I knew these were my last moments with him. I tried to memorize every detail about him. The creases between his eyebrows, his carefully styled brown hair, the laugh lines framing his face. There was no joy on his face now. Only fear and concern. For me.

War had been ravaging across the country for years. We thought that we were safe, that we could wait it out, but we were wrong. War was fast approaching our city.

Of course, the children were to be sent away, and even though I was technically eligible to join the army, my father wouldn't stand for it. I was being sent away too. We both knew that eventually the war would demand our country to draft men. My father, ever loyal to the nation, would volunteer. He'd never told me he would join the army, but I knew him too well.

In the fifteen years of my life, it had just been my father and I. I had his brown hair, but he told me that I had my mother's blue eyes. She had had flaming red hair and was lean and tall. My father said her smile could light up a room. Every time he told me about her, he described her as if she were an angel. She had died two days after giving birth to me. Sometimes, I couldn't help feeling that if I hadn't been born, she would still be here.

Pulling myself out of my thoughts, I focused again on my father. I couldn't help thinking about all the times he'd embraced me, comforted me, talked and laughed with me. He was my best friend, my mentor, my protector, my home. I couldn't handle the thought of having to be separated from him. If I kept thinking about leaving him, I knew I wouldn't be able to bear it. Suddenly, I felt tears welling up in my eyes. I turned and embraced him. I pressed my face into his shoulder and squeezed my eyes shut. He wrapped one arm around my back and held my head in his hand. I wouldn't cry. I wouldn't. If I did, I knew neither of us would let go.

"It's going to be alright," he murmured. We both knew that was a lie, but I nodded anyway. I only pulled away when I heard the conductor calling for the passengers. My father placed my bag into my hands and set his hands on my shoulders again. He looked into my eyes. I couldn't help noticing how worn he looked. Silver strands had been working their way into his hair lately and his eyes looked bloodshot and red from lack of sleep. Or from crying. I hoped it was the former. "We will see each other again," he said. "I promise you." All I could do was stare back. It was getting more and more difficult not to cry.

All I could think about was how everyone in our family was about to be separated. My mother, adrift somewhere in the afterlife, me, sent to some far away, foreign country, my father, to war. Like the seeds of a plant separated in the wind, or stars, hung in space. I could only hope my father and I would be reunited someday. I could only hope.

The conductor was giving his last call. I gave my father one last quick hug.

"Goodbye, Father," I said. I pulled away and looked up to him. "I hope you're right. I hope we do see each other again." He stared at me. He looked like he was trying to commit me to memory.

"I love you," he said.

"I love you, too." I couldn't hold it back anymore. One tear fell down my cheek. I turned and ran to the train. I hopped up to the steps right as the train started moving. I looked back to my father. All we could do was stare at one another. I thought of the times he helped me when I scraped a knee, the times we cooked meals together and laughed every time they turned out awful.

The tears came faster. I thought of when we would take walks through town in the middle of the night and pass through the park my mother had always loved. When we would go to the library, looking for any books that interested us. He always loved to read about geography. He'd wanted to travel around the world with me one day. I didn't know if that was ever going to happen now.

I could see tears on his face now too.

The smell of grease and oil burned my lungs and stung my eyes as the train started off. I watched my father until the train turned a corner, and he was gone. Now, I could only hope.

First Place Prose – Middle School
St. Francis Xavier, Petoskey

SLAM POETRY: 168 HOURS

JEFFREY KERR

I am not the product of bad parenting,

I am the product of half parenting.

Left my insufferable father at fifteen,
sixteen now with no remorse.

The last shot has blown through the barrel.

The guns I was given,

Just to keep me captive and entertained.

The only thing that he gave me was his name.

Jeffrey a godforsaken name provided by him.

Lynn, a feminine name for a male.

Kerr, the last thing I want to be.

Not anymore I am who I say I am.

I am Jeffrey.

Not the alcoholic or the angry fellow.

Not the one who lies straight to your face every time you ask.

I am the one who lends a hand to anyone in need.

The one who will be your friend

The one who wants to get involved with,

Politics,

Sports,

Hunting,

Fishing,

And overall

The one who cares for all life on earth.

As you can see I am not my radical Father.

Being locked in a room for a week.

Giving me plenty of time to think, reflect.

What else would one do with 168 hours?

Realize I am what I make myself to be.

I am made from my past.

I will become a man from what has occurred

And what is to come.

First Place Poetry – High School
Boyne City High School, Boyne City

JESUS IN THE BUBBLE BATH

KARAGAN ADAMS

We were so innocent. Our short blond hair that just barely covered our shoulders. We always tucked it behind our ears, sharing the space with the arms of our little round pink glasses. We were three years apart but our faces looked identical. Big blue eyes filled with wonder. Our skin was still new, free from imperfections that were soon to come. You were always so eager to learn.

You would learn something at Sunday school and couldn't wait to recreate it on me. Of course you being my sister I would let you do it without question. So when we were playing in the bath, fruity bubbles foaming around us, your face lit up with excitement as you retold me how Jesus healed the blind man with spit and mud at the pool. You were happy because our bath could be the pool. You told me I was the blind man, I took my little glasses off and shut my eyes super tight. I couldn't see anything but I listened to your familiar, loving voice talk through the story.

We didn't have mud, but you said your gum would do. You pulled it out of your mouth, I could smell the mint as cold hands smushed the gum onto my eyelids. You said it was perfect and that made me excited for the next step. You said that if you used real spit the gum wouldn't dry and I couldn't be healed, it made sense to me. Without warning the blackness went to red as your thumb put pressure over my eye. I reached up to feel what was there, on one eye there was something hard and round. I smell my hand. It smelled like spearmint but it had hints of metal to it. You told me it was a quarter and that I had to let it dry into the gum. We waited in silence. Our bath water was no longer warm and the bubbles had disappeared. Suddenly the bathroom door creaked open. "Hey, why is it so quiet in here?" Then Ma's voice went from questioning to an ungodly anger. She rips me from the tub and wraps me in a soft, fresh towel that smelled like flowers, it made me feel better than the cold water. She sat me on the sink and ran away. She returned with peanut butter. The creamy JIF filled my nose and made me hungry. She smeared it really thick over the gummy quarter and started to peel it off, yelling at you in the process. When Ma was done with my eye, she put me into the top bunk.

You lay in the bottom bunk weeping, because I had not been healed.

First Place Prose – High School
Harbor Springs High School, Harbor Springs

Contributors

Joyce Brinkman, Indiana Poet Laureate 2002-2008, believes in poetry as public art. She creates public poetry projects involving her poetry and the poetry of others. Her own poetry is on permanent display in a twenty-five foot stained glass window in an airport, in lighted glass artwork at a library and on a wall in the town square of Quezaltepecque, El Salvador. She is a founding board member of the not-for-profit organization Brick Street Poetry Inc. Joyce has received fellowships from the Mary Anderson Center for the Arts, the Vermont Studio and the Indianapolis Arts Council. Joyce has relatives in Michigan and loves visiting, particularly the Upper Peninsula. She is a graduate of Hanover College and lives in Zionsville, Indiana with her husband and a cantankerous cat.

Tim Chilcote is a freelance writer based in northern Michigan. His poetry and essays have appeared or are forthcoming in Gray's Sporting Journal, BULL Magazine, Art of Manliness, HOUR Detroit and other fine publications. Tim holds an MFA in creative writing from the University of Notre Dame.

Rick Fowler has had his articles published in a variety of magazines like Lake Superior Magazine, Michigan Out Door News, Woods-N-Water, Hook And Bullets, Mid West Outdoors, Mackinac Journal, Country Lines, and numerous newspapers. Growing up in Northern Michigan whet his appetite for fishing and hunting, which was further fueled by both his grandfather's, and his father's experiences in the outdoors. Rick writes about bird hunting and angling adventures in the Upper and lower Peninsulas. He has been a board member and vice-president of MOWA (Michigan Outdoor Writer's Association). A retired High School English teacher in Boyne City, Rick now devotes much of his free time away from assigning and correcting essays to writing his own.

A lifelong resident of Michigan, **CJ Giroux** teaches at Saginaw Valley State University, where he also serves as the assistant director of the school's writing center and its Center for Community Writing. He is also one of the founding editors of the community arts journal *Still Life.*

Grace Giroux lives in Saginaw, Michigan, where she is a senior in high school. Active in music and the arts, she plays piano, flute, and viola. One of her favorite places in the world is Leland, Michigan.

Steve Hooper writes songs for the Upper Peninsula by the name Under This Cold Sky. Born-and-raised a Yooper, he began writing songs about life in the U.P. and, upon spending several years in a "big" Midwestern city, subsequently longing to come back. Steve and his wife Sarah moved back home to the U.P. in 2016 and shortly after releasing an EP with songs about the history of the Marquette area and a full album celebrating the Great Lakes and life in the U.P. in 2018. Hooper places a strong emphasis on poetic songwriting and often perform at events alongside Upper Peninsula writers and poets.

Steven W. Huder is an amateur photographer with a passion for the woods and water of Northern Michigan. He lives in the Petoskey area.

Deda Kavanagh, a native Michigander, has spent 40 summers in Northern Michigan breathing clean, cool, lake-air. She was recently published in Bay Community Writing Center's, "Still Life", and her poetry collection, "Bicycle through a Covered Bridge", was published by Finishing Line Press.

Kelly Tingle Kazmierski is a multi-medium artist and creator of original and commissioned works of photography, pencil, pen and ink, acrylic, oil and mosaic. Kelly was an Art Prize 2016 finalist with a 16,000 piece collage 'Kelly's Kiss', and in 2017 published a children's book The Girl with Spaghetti Hair, which she is both the author and illustrator. In 2018, Harbor Springs Historical Society honored one of her heritage photographs. Born and raised in Windsor, Ontario, Kelly is a year-round resident of beautiful Harbor Springs, Michigan where her influences are rooted in the natural majesty of the Great Lakes and the purity of animals and nature. Here, surrounded by inspiration, is where she works from her studio above the shores of Little Traverse Bay.

John Lennon is an English Teacher in Northern Michigan. As a lover of music, nature, and people, he draws inspiration from all of the small wonders in the world that make life more meaningful.

Ellen Lord is a Michigan native. Her poetry has appeared in R.k.v.r.y Quarterly Literary Journal, Open Palm Print, Peninsula Poets chapbooks and Traverse Area District Library Poets Night Out chapbooks. She was the recipient of the Mike McGuire Poetry Prize in 2019. She won the Landmark Books Haiku Contest in 2017 & 2019. . She is a member of the Fresh Water Poets Group in Traverse City and the Charlevoices Writers' Group in Charlevoix. She is a behavioral health therapist.

Raymond Luczak grew up in Ironwood and Houghton, Michigan. He is the author and editor of 22 books, including Flannelwood (Red Hen Press). A proud Yooper, he lives in Minneapolis, Minnesota.

Helen Raica-Klotz is a writer living in mid-Michigan, trying to get back to her birthplace in the northern part of our state. She currently directs the Writing Center and Saginaw Bay Writing Project at SVSU, and has had twenty poems and memoir pieces published over the past ten years.

Charles Rammelkamp grew up downstate in Albion, Michigan and his family has owned property on Old Mission Peninsula for over 100 years. He presently lives in Baltimore, MD and comes to Michigan for two weeks every summer.

Greg Rappleye's work has appeared previously in Walloon Writers Review. His second collection of poems, A Path Between Houses (University of Wisconsin Press, 2000) won the Brittingham Prize in Poetry. His third collection, Figured Dark (University of Arkansas Press, 2007) was co-winner of the Arkansas Prize and was published in the Miller Williams Poetry Series. His fourth collection, Tropical Landscape with Ten Hummingbirds, was published in the fall of 2018 by Dos Madres Press. He teaches in the English Department at Hope College in Holland, Michigan.

Skip Renker spent all his early summers in Harbor Springs, MI, playing with friends and his eight siblings, later caddying and working in resort hotels. After several decades of teaching at Delta College in the Saginaw Valley, he now lives full time in Petoskey with his wife Julia Fogarty, also a former Delta College teacher. His poems have appeared in numerous journals and anthologies, including The Atlanta Review, Passages North, and Poetry Midwest, as well as in three books: Birds of Passage (Delta Press); Sifting the Visible (Mayapple Press); and Bearing the Cast (St. Julian Press).

Nancy Renko previously lived in Petoskey and worked as a Title IV tutor for Petoskey Public Schools. "It was my great pleasure to work with the Native American community and to gain an understanding of some of their traditions, lore, and history. The history behind story I have submitted has stayed with me for the past 50 years and I felt compelled to write it so that others may be reminded of the history of the Odawa people." After moving to Midland, MI, she continued her teaching career and retired in 2010, but has always treasured her memories of working with the Native American students in Petoskey.

Born in Pennsylvania, **David Anthony Sam** is the proud grandson of peasant immigrants from Poland and Syria. For much of his life, he lived and worked in the Detroit area, graduating from Eastern Michigan University (BA, MA) and Michigan State (Ph.D.). He lives now in Virginia with his wife and life partner, Linda. Sam's poetry has appeared in over 90 journals and publications and his poem, "First and Last," won the 2018 Rebecca Lard Award. He has five published collections including Final Inventory (Prolific Press 2018) and Finite to Fail: Poems after Dickinson, the 2016 Grand Prize winner of the GFT Press Chapbook Contest. A sixth, Dark Fathers, is forthcoming from Aldrich Press. He currently teaches creative writing at Germanna Community College, from where he retired as President in 2017. He serves as Vice President for the North Central Region of the Virginia Poetry Society.

Melissa Seitz has had her writing published in After: Stories About Loss & What Comes Next, The Bear River Review, The Dunes Review, The Lake, Walloon Writers Review, and other journals. Her photography has been published in Walloon Writers Review and Midwestern Gothic (online version). She lives with her husband in Higgins Lake, Michigan.

Jan Shoemaker's essay collection, Flesh and Stones: Field Notes from a Finite World, was published in 2016 and her poetry collection, The Reliquary Earth, was published early in 2019. Her work has been anthologized, featured on public radio, and has appeared in many magazines and journals.

Shelley Smithson resides both in Elk Rapids and in East Lansing, MI. She is a psychotherapist in East Lansing and enjoys writing in her free time. "Northern Michigan is often the setting that inspires me to take to pen (or pencil) and paper. She has been published in "The Sun" (published in Chapel Hill, N.C.) and her non-fiction essay about clinical practice was published in the creative journal of Olivet College, Olivet, Michigan, called "The Garfield Lake Review. Shelley is married, having raised a daughter and son and enjoy playing piano and doing volunteer work.

Phillip Sterling's books include the poetry collection And Then Snow, and, as editor, Isle Royale from the AIR: Poems, Stories and Songs from 25 Years of Artists-in-Residence (Caffeinated Press). A series of February poems, Short on Days, will be published by Main Street Rag as a chapbook in 2020.

Edy Stoughton has worn many hats in her life. She has been a teacher, head of a school and a social worker, raised 5 children and now is part of the lives of 6 grandchildren. She has a doctorate in education, and is an artist and a writer. "No part of my full life has given me as much joy as living on Sturgeon Bay in Northern Michigan where I am privileged to be part of all the moods of the lake, view thrilling sunsets and be refreshed by soft summer breezes."

Taylor Tucker graduated from the University of Illinois with a BS in Engineering Mechanics and is currently pursuing a Master's degree in Curriculum & Instruction. She has been published in the literary journal Talking River and currently writes for the university's Department of Mechanical Science and Engineering and has articles and an engineering blog published on their website and in seasonal magazines.

Edd Tury descended from Hungarian Gypsies. He is a Michigan native and avid Transcendentalist. His introversion often finds him exploring the wilderness on foot, bike or kayak. He enjoys writing and baking bread. He graduated from the University of Michigan during the turbulent sixties and continues to work as an electronics guru. His goal is to quit his day job and dance in the moonlight. Edd's writing has appeared in Dunes Review, Open Palm Print, Poet's Night Out chapbook, Detroit Metro Times, Michigan Out of Doors magazine, Michigan Woods n Waters, and the Ann Arbor News. Edd lives at the end of the road in Charlevoix County.

Steve Ullom watches life and writes from the middle of a continent with his wife and two dogs. His writing can be found at or is upcoming in Quail Bell Magazine, Allegro Poetry Magazine, Foliate Oak Literary Magazine, The Ravens Perch, Light – a Journal of Photography & Poetry, and Ascent, as well as in the anthologies The Colours of Refuge and Mytho.

Robert Vivian is the author of The Tall Grass Trilogy, Water And Abandon and two meditative essay collections, Cold Snap As Yearning and The Least Cricket Of Evening. His first poetry book is called Mystery My Country--and he's co-written a second called Traversings with the poet Richard Jackson. He teaches at Alma College and as a core faculty member at The Vermont College Of Fine Arts. His next book, coming out in 2020, is called All I Feel Is Rivers.

Glen Young is a teacher, writer, kayak guide, and house painter. His poetry has appeared in Walloon Writers Review, as well as the anthologies Beneath the Lilac Canopy and Thoreau at Mackinac. He is a founding member of the Foundation for Teaching and Learning, as well as the Little Traverse Literary Guild. He serves on the board of the Harbor Springs Festival of the Book and the Mackinac Arts Council. He divides his time between Petoskey and Mackinac Island in northern Michigan.

Amy Zaranek is an MFA student at Ashland University, where she is also the lead editor of creative nonfiction for The Black Fork Review. Her writing attempts to examine issues of sustainability and agriculture in contemporary America. She lives and writes in Northern Michigan.